GROUNDS FOR LOVE

A Divorce Lawyer's Guide to Rebuilding Your Confidence and Finding a Great Relationship

BY

PAUL ANTHONY RILEY

Table of Contents

Dedication v

Introduction vii

Chapter One: Men Cheat 1

    Grounds for Love Rule #1: Don't Blame Yourself. 4

    Grounds for Love #2: If Someone Tells You Who They Are, You Should Listen. 6

    Grounds for Love Rule #3: You Have to Identify the Players Early and Stay Away From Them. 10

    Grounds for Love Rule #4: Don't Ask Yourself Why. 14

    Grounds for Love Rule #5: Facebook Presents a Clear and Present Danger 29

    Grounds for Love Rule #6: Be a Co-Pilot Not a Passenger. 39

Chapter Two: Confidence Reboot 42

    Grounds for Love Rule #7: Stay Positive, This Too Shall Pass 46

Chapter Three: Moving On 58

    Grounds for Love Rule #8: Build it up slowly. 62

Grounds for Love Rule #9: Trust Your Instincts......................67
Grounds for Love Rule #10: Don't Settle. 76
Grounds for Love Rule #11: No Innuendo. 82
Grounds for Love Rule #12: Keep it hot. 84
Grounds for Love Rule #13: Be Your Man's Kate and Edith too..89

Legal Disclaimer 97

About the Author...99

Acknowledgements 101

Dedication

This book is dedicated to all the ex-wives and ex-girlfriends around the world who have had their hearts trampled in failed relationships.

Grounds for Love

Introduction

I shuffled from the courtroom, disheveled from what had been a confrontational and quite *un*-civil litigation regarding child support for my client and her three kids. I had always felt that the term *civil litigation* was an oxymoron, and no place is that more evident than divorce court.

As I made my way down the hallway, I replayed in my head the paragraphs of venom that had just been spewed, admittedly by both sides of the table.

My intention in these disputes is never to be combative but rather cordial and reasoned. However, I have come to realize that such strategy equates to bringing a knife to a gun fight.

In my experience, many divorce lawyers are overly aggressive and reluctant to end things in an expeditious way. Clearly, the more vicious and protracted the battle, the more money they make.

Grounds for Love

Generally speaking the only one who wins in a long, drawn-out divorce are the lawyers.

As I walked down the hallway I noticed an elevator in front of me, doors just about to close, I scrambled to get in.

The only other person on the ride down was an older lawyer I had seen around, he looked worse than I felt. The doors hadn't fully closed yet when he said, "I hate this shit. I have been a lawyer for 30 years; the only things I have done are criminal defence work and divorce. I'll take the criminals any day."

He went on, "At least with criminal defence, a guy comes to you and says, 'Hey I really screwed up, can you help me?' In divorce court, you have some guy coming to you, saying, 'I used to love her but I want you to really fuck her over!!' Or I have some woman coming to me saying, 'I want you to cut off his balls and feed them to him!!!'"

"Yeah", he said, "Give me the criminals."

Before the elevator hit ground floor my decision had been made. I had to write this book!

I had already been a doing this kind of work for years, but fortunately for me I realized that I had just taken a nine-story ride with the future…and it didn't look good.

Introduction

I no longer wanted to just be the guy at the end of these failed marriages, fighting over custody, money or the occasional Scottish terrier. Instead, I wanted to write this book to see if I could help prevent these vicious courtroom battles from ever occurring. Writing the book and laying out rules that can guide people, women particularly, in making better choices in deciding whom to partner with in life.

By making better choices at the beginning of the relationship, at least they would have a fighting chance of making it work, instead of ending up in a contentious, bitter and expensive divorce.

This book I write in particular for women, for two reasons. One, in my experience it's the man who screws up most marriages. Sorry fellas, it's the truth. Full disclosure, years ago I screwed up my own. And two, despite the fact that it's the guy who messed up, it's usually the woman who is left most hurt, emotionally damaged and devoid of self-confidence.

I'm writing this book not as a legal document. I'm certainly not dispensing legal advice here, but rather providing a raw, honest and hopefully at times humorous guide for women to make better choices in men, improve their relationship skills and also learn some integral strategies in keeping a man from straying.

I share all this from the perspective as a divorce lawyer and also from my own experiences in relationships and my own failed marriage.

In this book, I will make no excuses for men, but allow me to say this, rarely does anyone pull us aside in our youth and train us for relationships. Hardly, if ever, are we counselled at an early age as to how to treat women. The extent of the advice we get is; "don't hit girls" and "when they say no, its no." Tragically some guys don't even fully grasp that, as the #MeToo movement has well documented.

The rest of the time, as men, we are just winging it. Ladies you are literally handing your heart over to a dude who is flying blind, so inevitably there is a high likelihood that the relationship crashes.

My hope for you when you read you this book is that you will gain an insight into the minds of men and as a result navigate those potential pitfalls. If you have already been in a bad relationship…or two, then I hope you will take the lessons from this book, employ them and rebuild your confidence.

In this book, I will give you the Grounds for Love.

Chapter One

Men Cheat

Fuckhead

This first chapter could easily have been called 'men behaving badly', but instead of just pointing out the mistakes guys make, I ask them, as Jay Leno famously did of Hugh Grant, "What the hell were you thinking?!"

Years ago, a former client of mine stumbled into my office, he was distraught. He had found some text messages between his wife and someone who clearly seemed to be her lover.

LOVER: Babe, you on your way over?

WIFE: No, I can't make it. Fuckhead decided to cancel his fishing trip.

As my client continued to lament to me in my office, my mind wandered briefly as I couldn't help but think to myself:

- At some point in his relationship with his wife, he probably held doors open for her.
- At some point if she coughed late at night, he probably got out of bed to get her some water.
- At some point, he probably made love to her all night.

And at some point, someway, to her he became "Fuckhead".

During the lead-up to the divorce proceedings it was revealed that his wife did in fact seek comfort in the arms of another man, but only after she had found out that her husband had been cheating. Suspicious of his behavior she had hired a private investigator to follow him. Within a week and a half, the PI found that he was having affairs with, in no particular order, a neighbor, the nanny and one of his own cousins.

There are fundamental differences in the way males and females are driven, literally by their genetics. Having never been a woman, I can only truly give you the male perspective.

Men are driven to pursue, to capture. But once the deal is closed, we struggle with what's next. Even when they are in a committed, happy relationship guys tend to be hormonally driven for the hunt.

Men Cheat

One man in another divorce case explained that his wife was, "perfect, she's beautiful, I love hanging out with her and she would have sex everyday with me if I wanted."

Then why did you cheat?

"I just needed a little extra," he said.

Despite being admittedly happy, another woman giving him attention and wanting to have sex with him was apparently just too overwhelming for him to resist. He risked and lost everything for "a little extra".

He said, even while having sex with the other woman, he would think of the risk he was taking and while having sex he felt that the risk was worth it.

However, as soon as the sex was over and the rush dissipated, he could think more clearly and determine that maybe it wasn't worth it. This mental jousting between guilt and lust went on for months until the woman accidentally left a blonde wig under his car passenger seat. His wife came upon it when the blonde hairs tickled her ankles as the couple were on their way out to dinner.

Dinner got cancelled. The marriage too.

Grounds for Love Rule #1: Don't Blame Yourself.

If you get cheated on, you have to treat it as what it is. Someone else did something harmful at your expense, but it's not a reflection of who you are or your worth.

A large part of my time spent as a divorce lawyer is in the company of people who have recently had their trust breached. As a result, I am often thrust into the role of confidence coach, trying to help rebuild their self-esteem after they have had their hearts broken and they see their worlds coming apart.

The first thing I encourage people in that position to do is to create a "Why I am Great" list, putting down on paper all the positive things about themselves and their lives; achievements, friendships, etc.

When you find out you have been cheated on would be an ideal time to pull out such a list or to make one. You have to remind yourself that you are awesome and that the way you are feeling right now will pass. Keep in mind that many people go through this experience and come out better still. You need to remind yourself that lots of awesome, beautiful and talented women have been cheated on and they are still awesome, beautiful and talented. Don't let the weakness of another person derail your life for too long.

Every single day, millions of people get cheated on. Every single day. This is not unique behaviour and is no reflection on you.

Now is a time for positive self-talk. Remind yourself how fabulous you are. Motivate yourself with positive affirmations. Don't fall victim to that negative voice in your head.

The moment there is even an inclination for negative talk, you have to remind yourself of your Great List, stay positive and champion yourself. This is extremely important and it works. If you say the positive affirmations enough, your mind will adopt it and believe it as so. Even when you are feeling your worst, it's been well documented that positive self-talk can heal your spirits, if repeated enough.

It's part of the human condition to be tough on ourselves, but when you are down, as you would be after finding out you have been cheated on, it's definitely not the time to engage in self-criticism. Stay up. Stay positive.

Grounds for Love #2: If Someone Tells You Who They Are, You Should Listen.

The hormonal battle is one that guys will acquiesce to. Clearly this is not unique to divorce clients. Numerous psychological studies have shown that men who cheat often say they felt "overwhelmed with desire at the time". Couple that with the ability to rationalize their actions by leaning on societal perceptions. Take for example Joss Whedon, the producer and writer of the '90s television show *Buffy the Vampire Slayer.* Recently his ex-wife Kai Cole wrote on a blog post that during their sixteen-year marriage Whedon cheated on her with actresses, friends, fans and co-workers. She went further, saying that when she confronted him about it, he rationalized the affairs by saying, "In many ways I was the height of normal, in this culture. We are taught to be providers and companions and at the same time, to conquer and acquire—specifically sexually—and I was pulling off both".

Whedon may sound like a jerk, but only because he is voicing what a lot of men quietly think. There is clearly a historical difference in how sexual behavior is perceived regarding men and women. It hasn't changed since the beginning of time, despite the efforts of TV shows like Sex in the City. A man who has sex with a lot of women or who has sex outside of a committed relationship is just "being a man". If a woman pulls that stunt, then she is often seen as a slut.

The irony is, some men love those so-called sluts. They just don't generally marry them, but they'll sleep with them often at the expense of their wives. This is historically known as the Madonna-Whore complex. Originally identified by Sigmund Freud back in the day, the theory is that generally speaking, men class women into two categories, Pure and Whore.

I had a client who was a former pro athlete. He admitted he had a great wife that he adored, yet he couldn't stay out of the strip clubs. He had a long-term affair with one particular dancer who knew he was married but resigned herself to being the 'other woman'. In fact, she felt she had the better role. She would tell him that "I would rather be the other woman, than the woman being lied to".

One day he went to the strip club to meet her, she wasn't there. After he waited a few minutes inside, he exited the club to leave, only to find a crowd gathered around his shiny silver Porsche.

There... standing on the hood of his car was his dancer, dressed as she always was at work, in nothing but a white business shirt and red pumps.

She was armed with an aluminum baseball bat and was repeatedly smashing down on the windshield of his car.

The glass cracked, displaying what looked like an elaborate spider web woven fully across it.

Unsatisfied that the windshield, though shattered had remained intact, the dancer then proceeded to maniacally stomp on the glass until one of her heels pierced it and got stuck.

After unsuccessfully trying to pry the shoe free a couple of times, she calmed down, adjusted her business shirt and gracefully removed her foot from what was now a windshield ornament.

As my client looked on in shock and embarrassment, she stepped down from the car, dropped the bat and still wearing one heel, lopsidedly strutted past him back to the strip club as the crowd parted for her and cheered.

Men Cheat

The stripper in the business shirt had found out that my married client had been having an affair with yet another dancer in the same club, at the same time.

Once the crowd dispersed, he was left to drive the car to a nearby garage with the red high heel still stuck in the windshield. The way it was imbedded in the glass he feared if he yanked it out the whole windshield would have caved in.

The stripper in the white business shirt didn't stop there, she would later send explicit pictures of her and my client to his now ex-wife.

I would later ask him, "if you say your wife is perfect, why the strippers?"

"Because they are freaks" he said. "…and they'll do things my wife won't."

He hadn't asked his wife to do the things the strippers did, he just determined, "she's not that type of girl."

A lot of men think that to get both types of women, you need more than one woman.

Grounds for Love Rule #3: You Have to Identify the Players Early and Stay Away From Them.

This is not a book on bashing men, clearly or I'd be beating up myself, but some guys are just unsalvageable.

There is a great scene in the movie The Dark Knight. It's Alfred the butler's seminal scene in the film. Bruce Wayne is trying to make sense of his arch-rival the Joker and Alfred says, "Some men aren't looking for anything logical like money. They can't be bought, bullied, reasoned or negotiated with. Some men just wanna watch the world burn."

In the spirit of that, I would suggest to you that, some men can't be managed, fixed, satiated or satisfied. Some men are just players who leave a train wreck of heartache in their wake.

The only thing to do with guys like that is to identify them early before you are emotionally invested and stay clear of them. You can't help them. You will literally waste years of your life on that futile endeavor.

Men Cheat

Because of the nurturing nature of women, they often think they can change men. They meet someone who they know is not exactly right for them, but they think they will be the one to turn him around. Or, they know the guy has been a bit of a wild man, but they make the assumption that he will be different once he gets involved with them. This is rarely the case.

Several years ago, there was this off-off Broadway play called, 'I Met You, I Love You, Now Change.' I think many women go into relationships with that attitude, when in reality, no-one can change anyone. People struggle to change themselves, much less someone else being able to compel them to evolve, unless its something *they* truly want to do.

Some guys are just wired to run game on every woman who enters their ecosystem. You can have your fun with guys like that, but if you choose to get into a serious relationship with someone like that then you are inviting heartache to your doorstep.

I had a client who when she met her husband he had been a notorious wild man. His business was bringing in musicians to perform at various nightclubs around the city. He literally worked most nights until 5 am. He essentially threw parties for a living and made good money doing so.

She assumed because he told her he loved her and had a child with her that this party animal would somehow become someone else. Even before they got married she started hearing repeated rumors that he was sleeping with half the waitresses at the various clubs where he worked. He consistently denied it. She chose to believe him every time.

One day she had to go pick him up from the local hospital. He had fallen asleep in one of his lover's beds. The problem was, his lover's ex-boyfriend still had a key to her place, showed up unannounced and proceeded to pummel him awake. He had to run out of the apartment in nothing but his underwear. He had to wait downstairs, outside the building, in the winter, for the ambulance to pick him up.

He wasn't hurt too badly; the marriage however was destroyed and my client's confidence shattered.

At one of the settlement conferences leading up to the divorce, he looked at my client and said, "You knew exactly what you were getting into when you married me."

I really don't think she did, or at the very least didn't want to. She wanted to believe the guy would change. She believed in the redeeming powers of love. That was a mistake. I couldn't really blame the guy for what happened in this case. He came as advertised.

In the case of the guy with the red pump stuck in his windshield, his wife knew that he frequented strip joints. He did so when he was an athlete and he kept doing so after he retired. Her theory was, she wasn't going to try and change him. He was there every single week, but somehow she didn't think that he would become involved with a stripper? Or two?

I believe in that situation she was willfully blind about the strip clubs and what could potentially be going on there. However, she felt that he crossed a line when pictures started showing up in her email. Seeing pictures of your spouse with his lover is not a punishment I would wish on anyone. You can't un-see that once you have seen it.

The great sex therapist Esther Perel calls catching your lover cheating in the digital age, "death by a thousand cuts". I would tend to agree.

Grounds for Love Rule #4: Don't Ask Yourself Why.

This is not the question to ask. You know why. He cheated because he wanted to. It's that simple. Most guys will cheat if given the chance and they think they can get away it. Some men will cheat even when they know they are taking a risk and there is a chance they may get caught.

The problem with asking "Why" is that invariably the answer that may come back could entail placing some blame at your own feet. No blame should reside with you. Men cheat simply because they want to. You have to accept that and work on healing and moving on.

The hurt is real and you will want to replay every lie you think he may have told you. If you have seen text messages or digital photos, you will continually replay those in your mind as well. All of this will elongate your suffering. Don't ask yourself why. Don't ask him why. Accept that he cheated on you and move on. Looking back and trying to diagnose the root of the infidelity is truly futile.

Your focus should be on repairing your self-esteem and rebuilding your confidence. Lamenting "why" is the antithesis of that.

You need self-confidence to feel empowered and its only by being empowered that you can successfully move on and hopefully find a better relationship or situation.

It's a War Out There:

One client I had, explained his repeated infidelity like this. He said, "Its a war out there. Women know a guy is married and they still are willing to give it up to him. It's a war." This is not novel, the married guy putting the blame for his infidelity not on himself, but rather on the women he is cheating with.

Well, if it is a war, quite often the home team is losing. Some surveys estimate that 44% of men in committed relationship cheat. I would argue that its higher than that. Some guys are so secretive about their infidelity that they won't even admit it on an anonymous survey.

Most of the time the 'other' woman knows that the guy is married or in a committed relationship.

Occasionally though some guys *will* try to string along more than one woman without either knowing about the other, but I

Grounds for Love

think that's rare. It's just too much work for men to have different women out there thinking that each of them is the only one. But admittedly it does happen. I've even heard stories about guys being married to one woman AND engaged to someone else.

One of my best friends was a reporter for a major media company. She started dating a cop. Very early into the relationship her instincts told her that he was a player. Being a really good reporter, it didn't take her long to figure it out. It wasn't hard really. She placed one phone call to the police station where he worked. The cop who answered the phone was only too happy to tell her everything she wanted to know.

My friend simply said, "Hey, I'm dating (so and so) and I just want to know if any other women call there looking for him." The cop on the phone gleefully proceeded to give her names and numbers of all the other women who called. He even told her which ones called most frequently.

When my friend told me about this, I said, "just forget about the guy". I told her, "you are not far into the relationship, you haven't invested much emotionally, just walk away, let someone else deal with him".

Men Cheat

She wouldn't have it. After all, journalists are supposed to 'fight the good fight.' She wanted to take him down, "for the sisterhood". She proceeded to call all of the other women. I think there were seven of them, including one who was the guy's wife and one who was the guy's fiancée.

She then arranged to have dinner with him at a local restaurant for six pm. She had invited all of the other women to show up there at five.

When he walked in, they were all there. It wasn't a good scene as he was fully exposed.

The cop didn't take what my friend did very kindly. In fact, shortly thereafter, her property was vandalized. She assumed it was him. Later still, the cop pulled her over on some trumped up traffic violation, hand resting on his gun the whole time, menacing her.

I don't know what he was thinking, she had a whole media company behind her. Her and the company reported him and the cop ended up losing his job.

Despite my friend's epic takedown, at least two of the women who showed up that day kept seeing the guy. Even after the whole charade had been exposed they didn't value themselves enough or maybe they lacked the self-esteem to leave the relationship, even though it had been built on a foundation of fraud, misdirection and lies.

Admittedly this cop was an outlier, because to pull off a scheme like that was literally a full-time job.

The red flags would have been there, but many women are trusting and probably weren't looking for any signs.

This is how the cop pulled it off. From before he married his wife, he told her that police officers worked 12-hour shifts. That was a lie that bought him four extra hours every night to do whatever he wanted.

So, he had a home with his wife and child.

He also had an elderly father who lived in a house in the same city. He kept a room there and told the fiancée that his father's home belonged to him. So, she thought, 'what a great dude, letting his elderly dad live with him'.

Then he had another bunch of women that he would see at their own places or occasionally he would bring one of them to his father's house. The old man was probably glad for the company.

I'm exhausted just writing this guy's story. I don't know how he pulled it off, but he was engaged for a couple years while married, so this was no short term set up.

Most guys are not that crazy. Nor do men want to work that hard to cheat.

Men Cheat Based on The Opportunity

Years ago, in one of his standup routines, comedian Chris Rock famously said "Men cheat based on the opportunity. Recently Rock divorced. It was revealed that while married he carried on numerous affairs. Clearly the opportunities presented themselves.

There are probably as many theories as to why men cheat, as there are men cheating.

If you pick up any psychology magazine they will have a list of top ten reasons. Pick up another magazine, they will list ten more.

Quite frankly, I think the comedian wasn't too far off. The bottom line is this, most guys will cheat if they think they can get away with it. Not all men. But most.

As I stated earlier. It is estimated that about half the men and quarter of the women in committed relationships cheat. Women are more inclined to cheat for emotional attachment. Men overwhelmingly cheat for the sex and the excitement. Most of these men will tell you that they love their wives and are not trying to intentionally blow up their marriage, but they get caught up in lust and just roll with desire.

I had one client of mine, who was caught having sex with a co-worker on a work trip. Word spread to his wife and she filed for divorce.

When I asked him how he could take a risk like that, especially around people who knew him *and* his wife, the business leader looked me in the eyes and said of the hook up, "I don't know, I had a couple of drinks and all of a sudden it felt like her and I were all that mattered." Ridiculous. At the time, all that mattered was having sex with somebody different.

Men just don't look at sex the same way women do. There needs to be very little emotional capital invested for us to have sex with a woman.

I remember being out with a very elegant and sophisticated young woman many years ago. She would eventually grow to be a well-known journalist. One evening she was out with me and the cast of characters I used to hang out with.

When one friend revealed that he had only ever had one-night stands and had never been in a real relationship, she was shocked.

"How could you just keep having sex with people you didn't really like?" She asked.

"Like them?" He said. "I don't even know them,"

She was the only woman out with us that evening, having dinner with five men. She was also the only person even remotely shocked by what my friend had just said.

During the same dinner, another one of the guys told a story about how he had started dating this woman for a couple of months, more so just hooking up with her for sex once a week than dating.

One evening she was supposed to come over for their weekly hook-up, but due to bad weather she called him to cancel. He ended up speaking to her on the phone for over an hour. Realizing that this was really the first time he had an extended conversation with her, he asked her, "So, did you grow up here?"

"No, I'm from Halifax, Nova Scotia." She said.

"Oh! I went to college there. Where did you go to school?"

"I went to St. Mary's University." She said.

"Oh! I went to school across town at Dalhousie. What part of the city did you live?"

"I lived in Fenwick Towers." She said.

Grounds for Love

"Really? I lived around the corner from there. Wait. Did I fuck you back in Halifax?"

"Yes. You did." She said.

"I been seeing you for over a month, why didn't you tell me?"

"Ah, what was I supposed to say? Hi, you fucked me years ago, but clearly you don't remember?"

Sex is just not as important for men. Let me be clear. It's important in terms of a pursuit, a conquest, but for lots of guys it often holds very little emotional value.

I would venture to guess that there are not too many women who will have sex with a guy and years later meet the guy again and start having sex with the same guy, without knowing she had already had sex with the guy in the first place.

Men can do that.

However, while sex is easy for men, most of us will struggle within the confines of a relationship. Not all, but most.

Men want the relationship and it's important to us, but it conflicts with the desire to hunt and to conquer.

As Esther Perel says, "How can you desire what you already have?"

So, men cheat.

Here a Cheat, There a Cheat:

There are basically four different types of cheaters. Every man who cheats fall into one of the following categories:

The Perpetual Cheater:

This is a guy who has never really bought into the idea of a committed relationship. He goes along with it because he is socialized to believe that the best place for a man after a certain age, is to 'settle down' with one woman. He may subscribe to the relationship, but he never really commits to it. He has no desire to be monogamous and just looks for ways to circumvent the deal.

This guy doesn't feel bad when he cheats. He feels he is being who he is supposed to be. He loves having the wife at home, while he still gets to do what he wants. There is a sense of entitlement as he feels he deserves to have more than one woman. He thinks being monogamous is for suckers.

This guy actively pursues cheating opportunities and he covers his tracks well. He is the type of guy who is inclined to use cheating websites to look for women.

On his phone, he'll have the cheating apps. There is a whole industry of cheating apps to accommodate this guy and his many transgressions.

I don't advise you looking through anyone's phone, but if you are going down that road, some of the apps to be aware of are:

Various Private Photo Apps: They are password protected and keep private pictures secured as opposed to in the phone's normal photo library.

Private Message Apps: numbers are added as a 'private' contact and messages go directly into the app as opposed to the phone's general inbox. Some renditions even delete all messages when the phone is shaken. So, if you walk into a room and your man starts shaking his phone, it's not his way of trying to get a better cell signal.

There are even counter intelligence apps which allow the cheater to leave his phone unattended and if you try to snoop through it, it takes a picture of you from the front camera. One of the key signs that your man may be up to no good, is if he never lets his phone out of his hands. This app allows him to at least give the impression that he has nothing to hide.

There are countless other apps and they are all made for the perpetual cheater.

The Occasional Cheater:

This guy will cheat if the opportunity presents itself. Unlike the perpetual cheater, this guy does not go looking for action elsewhere, but if he's on a business trip or out on a 'boys weekend' and there is an attractive woman who is into it, he'll cheat.

He gets caught up in the moment and just goes along with it. This guy feels remorse after the fact, but only after and only for a little while.

The occasional cheater won't come home and confess to anybody. Kind of like "whatever happens in Vegas, stays in Vegas", he is ok with keeping it a secret and he is ok with doing it again. This guy doesn't keep up long term affairs. He thinks the commitment he made to his partner is important, but he doesn't feel he has to be perfect in terms of his fidelity.

He rationalizes it by thinking that as long as his affairs are not frequent and he doesn't get involved with anyone on a long-term basis then he is doing his part. Like the perpetual cheater, this guy doesn't believe that its realistic for a man to be with just one woman, but for the most part he tries to honor his commitment.

If occasionally he cheats. He can live with that. This guy is the toughest guy to catch cheating because it rarely happens and its usually when he is away from home. He doesn't normally carry on communication much after the fact so the sloppy clues that are at times present with the Perpetual Cheater, are not apparent here.

The Emotional Cheater:

This guy gets caught up emotionally with his lover on the side. Of all the types of cheaters, this guy is most likely to be caught. His emotions affect his ability to hide his infidelity. This is the guy who will be texting in the bathroom and checking messages *while* in bed with you. He not only has sex with the woman on the side, but he often falls in love with her too. He is not as random as the previous two cheaters. He is more likely to get involved with someone he knows or use to know.

Arguments are more likely to occur with this type of cheater because in his mind, he feels as though the other woman understands him better. While the previous two other cheaters mentioned, compartmentalize their affairs, this guy allows the affair with the other woman to seep into his committed relationship. He changes his daily routine and has unpredictable mood swings.

Numerous clients of mine say they would start fights with their spouse on purpose just to give them a reason to storm out of the house and go see their lover.

The Emotional Cheater is always looking for excuses to leave the house because he has grown attached to the woman on the side. He takes more risks and seeks more privacy so he can make calls and check messages. Clues to look for are; He is all of a sudden spending more time texting and he is spending a lot more time chatting online, usually in a different room.

This is also the cheater that is influenced most by the woman on the side. He may exhibit new interests in different types of music and his stories become inconsistent in terms of where he's been and with whom.

The Oops I Cheated Cheater:

Generally speaking this guy doesn't cheat. He made a mistake and now struggles with whether to confess to you or not.

This guy is normally a solid guy in terms of being loyal in his relationship. This type of cheating tends to be a one-off. In fact, twenty five percent of men who cheat say it was a one time occurrence. That's this guy.

He's not going to cheat with some random woman, its normally someone he knows.

This guy isn't the type to creep around online. His misdeed is more likely to occur on a work trip.

Fifty five percent of men who cheat say they are happy in their marriage.

Grounds for Love Rule #5: Facebook Presents a Clear and Present Danger

Facebook has facilitated enough infidelity to make Ashley Madison blush.

Back in the day if you had a high school girlfriend or a college sweetheart they came into your life and then they went. With Facebook, nobody is ever gone for very long.

You just enter their name in the search and twenty years vanishes, here they are.

A client came to me after her husband filed for divorce. Everyone who knew them thought they were the perfect couple and in fact if you checked their Facebook you would often see pictures of them fawning over each other. To the world they were perfectly happy. With their three young kids, a dog and a cat, they were the envy of their neighborhood friends.

The problem was, the year before, she had received a Facebook friend request from her college boyfriend from twenty years ago, a guy who she'd apparently never gotten over and she proceeded to tell him as much.

Within two days of the friend request she was holed up in a crappy hotel room having sex with him.

It became a monthly thing, only in better hotels.

To her, this was the guy she should have been with her whole life. She had always known that and now spending this time with him only confirmed it.

She said he made her feel "ways her husband never could" and she decided she had to have this relationship with him.

He was also married and both of them had no intentions of leaving their marriage and children. They kept seeing each other for a year, even escaping away for the occasional night together.

One night her husband found some messages on her Facebook and the whole thing was exposed. That was the end of the idyllic enviable marriage.

Twenty years ago, marriages didn't have to contend with social media and online dating sites. Technology has indeed been a game changer in terms of dating and mating. Never has it been easier to meet someone and start up a relationship and it's not just for sex, countless people have found true love online. Years ago people would hide the fact that they met online. It's no longer a practice that people feel embarrassed to admit. The opposite in fact. Every year more and more people are looking for love in all the online places.

The flip side of that is, never has it been easier to cheat on your spouse and there is no sign of that slowing down either.

A recent survey of divorce lawyers in the United States found that sixty six percent of them had used evidence from Facebook in a recent divorce proceeding.

Forty one percent of cheaters surveyed said that Facebook was the reason they got caught.

Facebook provides the most conducive atmosphere online to hook up with people for an affair. There are no strangers on your Facebook. You know everyone. In some cases, they may be people you dated in the past or people you may have wanted to date but circumstances didn't allow it.

Staring at a bunch of pictures of someone you were in love with years ago can't possibly be good for your present relationship, especially if you are currently going through stress with your current partner, but lots of people do it.

What may start as an innocent text or friend request, then leads to pictures being perused, then soon clandestine late-night chat sessions with someone they remember from when times were easier and stress free and good.

If they are not already online friends, guys just search them up and send a request and at times within minutes there is a response.

As another client who was caught carrying on several affairs on Facebook said, "On Facebook you are fucking the familiar. Unlike those cheating websites where you never know what kind of weirdo you might meet."

Guys don't read innuendo very well. You have to be explicit. You have to let them know how important fidelity is to you. Don't assume they will hold it in the same regard. I have heard from countless men who thought their wives would have been upset at them for cheating, but they didn't think their wives would leave them because to them, sex with someone else was "just sex". The men didn't think it was important enough to end a marriage or a family over.

In many cases the 'infidelity conversations' were never had, it was just assumed.

In most cases it was the wrong assumption.

As anyone who has been the victim of a cheating spouse will tell you, it's not just the sex that's hurtful. It's the time the cheater spent building a relationship with someone else. It's the lying and deception. It's the intimacy created with another while the relationship at home had flatlined, desperate for some resuscitation of its own.

Though it may seem like stating the obvious, rules that govern the relationship have to be explicitly communicated to men. The same thing applies to online behavior. You have to let men know what the expectations are regarding Facebook and any other online activity. If it goes unsaid, guys will take shelter under the ambiguity.

It's simple really. If a guy is in a committed relationship, he shouldn't be communicating with old girlfriends on his Facebook. He shouldn't be communicating with them on the down low. It's the same as having lunch or dinner with an old lover every week or every night, yet lots of guys do it.

Facebook is just too tempting a proposition for even the most committed individuals.

Too many guys use Facebook as a dating site. They conjure up past lovers, find out about their 'situation' and if there is even the slightest opening, the pursuit is on.

We have already discussed how much guys love to pursue. What better to pursue than someone you had already conquered before and haven't been with in a while. It's like new and familiar all in one. As a result, men love the Facebook hook-up.

You have to set the ground rules regarding Facebook. I am not suggesting that you have to demand that your man gets off Facebook all together, but certainly there have to be parameters. He shouldn't be sending out friend request to past lovers or potential new conquests. Would he like to know that half your friends on Facebook are past lovers? NO. Then he should respect your wishes as well.

It has to be non-negotiable, you can't be committed and still be running rampant on Facebook. Nothing good is going to come from that. If the guy uses Facebook in the right way, then no problem. But if it's used to keep tabs on past lovers or to send out a random friend request because he sees an attractive woman online. That's just asking for trouble.

Some male clients of mine avoid Facebook at all cost. In fact, they call it Bustedbook and for that reason they refuse to get a Facebook account because they don't want to put themselves in a precarious position. Some of them have a past and they don't necessarily want that past finding them on Facebook and trying to start up conversations.

Let your man know what the guidelines are. This has to be done early in the relationship. Facebook has to be discussed. The rules governing Facebook have to be clearly defined by both sides. Unlike cheating websites, Facebook is something that is out there in the open and people don't hide to use it. It allows for cheating in plain sight.

Winging It:

There is no school course given to young people early on as to how to maintain a solid relationship. That is an assumed role of parents, but most times the parents themselves are overwhelmed trying to make sense of their own marital issues. They hardly have time to teach someone else, when they are struggling themselves. Further, with most marriages now ending in divorce, its more than likely that any example a young kid sees growing up is not an ideal one.

Even in great homes with tight families it's rare that a young person gets the kind of conversation from their parents as to how to maintain love, trust and respect during the tough years that most marriages inevitably go through.

Even good couples crumble under unforeseen pressures that were never anticipated as they stood in front of friends and family and professed undying love for each other.

In my case, I was fortunate enough to marry a great girl who I had dated for years.

Within a year of the marriage, Liza and I bought a house, had a son and I started my law practice. Fifteen months later we added a daughter.

Within a couple of years into the marriage, a business opportunity presented itself that had me working in New York State, three days a week. Going from Toronto to New York every week for almost a year, leaving my young wife with two small kids.

I was the key man in raising money to take a company public. I raised over eight million dollars from venture capitalists in Los Angeles and New York for the initiative. I also invested quarter million dollars of our money and investments from friends as well.

It was great for a while as things went exactly according to plan. I especially felt great about giving my friends this chance to make money as the stock price climbed. Then the market crash of 2007-08 hit. Within days the fledgling company was worthless. We lost all the money and almost lost our house.

During this whole debacle, I never talked to my wife about it. I just kept trying to right the ship by myself. Spending more time away, doing everything I could to salvage something from the company, to no avail.

Now, I consider myself a pretty reasonable person. Yet I never once looked at my wife and told her exactly where things were.

Liza is probably the antithesis of me when it comes to taking risks. She has had one job since she graduated University. She has worked in sales for a major tech company and yearly is always one of their top people. She would have had some good insight for me. She could have provided some good counsel. Instead, I alienated myself from her and in the process, I let the relationship wither.

With the business failing in such a spectacular way, I felt as though I had let her down. Maybe there was some guilt there. I knew there was some shame as well because this was the first time I had lost at anything so significant. I had not only lost our money, but money that friends invested as well. This was the most painful time I had ever endured.

Instead of going home to my wife and regrouping. I looked elsewhere to soothe my hurt. I went where there were no obligations, no expectations. I just looked-for pleasure to mask my disappointment. Shortly thereafter Liza and I divorced.

As men, we are raised to tough things out. It starts at an early age. I perpetuate it myself. When my young daughter would stumble and fall, I'd run to pick her up. Conversely, when the boy fell, I would say, "Get up man!"

I coach my son's youth basketball team now and I see it manifest itself during every game. We coach the kids to be tough. Parents yell from the stands at the young boys if they show even a glimmer of frailty. So, we grow up as men being tough. Not crying. Not complaining. And certainly not running to our wives for help. That would have been a sign of weakness. Instead I toughed it out and sought comfort in the arms of other women, at the expense of my wife and kids.

Grounds for Love Rule #6: Be a Co-Pilot Not a Passenger.

Don't leave all the navigating of the relationship to the man. Be a co-pilot in directing where you want it to go. Don't be a passenger on a cross Atlantic flight. Be more like a generous driving instructor. Let him take the wheel sure, as men we need to feel as though we are the ones driving, but be by his side gently providing guidance in terms of where you want the relationship to go. And if need be, you may have to grab the wheel and quickly jolt right or left. Then when its safe, hand him back the wheel again, but always stay alert on your ride together.

A guy trying to lose weight will hire the best fitness coach he can find. If he runs a business, he will align himself with the best business coach or mentor he can discover. But regarding his relationship, guys rarely seek any advice. We just wing it. We are literally making it up as we go along.

The most important relationship in our lives, but we are reluctant to talk to anyone else about it, even if we feel it's in trouble. We won't even talk to the woman who is in the relationship with us, much to our detriment.

I had one client who started a company and it was doing well. As it started to grow, he hired one of his best friends who was an accountant to handle all financial matters. My client's focus was in growing the company and he was successful in doing so. He left all money matters to be handled by his friend the accountant.

My client's wife kept asking him, "who is backing up the accountant to make sure he is handling things appropriately?" My client was offended that she would suggest that his best friend would do anything to harm him or the company. They argued over it on numerous occasions until finally she relented and didn't raise the issue anymore.

A couple of years into the business, they found out the accountant had been embezzling funds. By the time they found out, it was too late to save it. They lost the company. They divorced as a result.

The ironic part was, he actually was the one who filed for divorce. When I asked him why, he said, "She has lost confidence in me and I just can't live with that."

Really what he was saying was, the shame of having cost his family so much was too much for him. Every time he looked at his wife he felt pain. Every time they argued, she would bring up the financial loss they suffered.

Nobody trains us for this. Our motivation as men is to provide for and protect our family. When we feel we are dropping the ball, it's painful.

When a guy feels he is letting down the relationship by not doing his part, he is less inclined to want to discuss it. Men don't generally communicate during those times. He will more likely withdraw and isolate himself. This will also be one of the times he will look for distractions elsewhere to help him forget about the issues at home.

Let him have his space, but let him know you are there and available for him to discuss things with when he wants. Don't press, just showing that you are still supportive is enough.

With his confidence already down, now is not the time to pile on. He will only withdraw further.

Chapter Two

Confidence Reboot

Cheated On, Now What?

A lovely woman walked into my law office about 8 years ago. She was intelligent, stylish and clearly successful. She sat down in our conference room and told me that I needed to get her out of her marriage "post haste".

She proceeded to tell me that her husband had done nothing wrong, that he was a great guy. She had a twelve-year-old daughter with him and their life together had been really good.

Then she said she had been cheated on, not by the husband but by the man she was in love with before she had met her husband.

For fifteen years she had been carrying around the remnants of that prior relationship. For fifteen years she had been unable to trust a man. She married her husband and admitted he was a great guy, but because of what happened to her with her old boyfriend, she still couldn't bring herself to fully trust and it was eating away at her marriage.

The effects of being cheated on can be devastating to anyone. Infidelity is so pervasive in our society that we tend to think, "OK, cheated on? Brush yourself off and keep it moving."

However, to many women it is not so easy to get past a betrayal by a lover who looked them in the eyes told them they loved them more than anything in the world, then went out and broke their trust. Sometimes the damage is devastating and the pain long lasting.

My client went on to tell me that even fifteen years later and even though it had nothing to do with him, every time her husband leaves the house to go on a work trip she feels sick with fear that he will cheat. After a decade and a half of this and numerous therapy sessions, she has decided that her best recourse is to divorce him and not be in any committed relationship. "Maybe I'll just date people online, guys who live far away so I don't grow too attached." She said.

Being cheated on can literally make people sick. Some women describe being violently ill after they found out. Digital technology makes it even worse, as now you no longer speculate as to what your partner may or may not have done or said to his lover, quite often the evidence is painfully right there for you to see. Text messages, digital photos, it all adds up to an agonizing ordeal. The feeling of betrayal and rejection used to be hard enough, now women often have the dialogue of messages in front of them.

Finding out your man has cheated, is a direct shot to your self-esteem. When this happens, many women look at themselves as the reason why the guy strayed. They think, "Maybe I am not pretty enough, or sexy enough." Or perhaps they think, the other woman "may be more intelligent or sophisticated" or a "better lover". All of this self-doubt leads to serious damage being done to one's self-confidence.

But before we go any further, allow me to offer you a brief list of women who its well established in the public domain that they have been cheated on:

Jennifer Garner;

Halle Berry;

Gwen Stefani;

Demi Moore;

Maria Shriver; and

Hillary Clinton

No one would suggest that those women lack beauty, intellect or sophistication. Those are powerful, successful and attractive women.

As I stated earlier in the book, men have affairs very rarely based on the fact that their partner is lacking in something. Men have affairs because they want to. We have the desire and at times we make the decision to succumb to those desires.

But when you find out that you have been cheated on, none of this matters. You are devastated and most women will look at themselves as having failed the relationship somehow.

As I said earlier, the first thing you have to do is absolve yourself from any responsibility in the affair. You can't take responsibility for someone else's actions. I am not saying that women are blameless in the erosion of every relationship, but if there are problems there should be communication. If your partner deals with stress in the relationship by going off and having an affair, you can't wear that.

Further, being cheated on does not make you uniquely flawed, in fact it makes you closer to the norm. As we have discussed, affairs are rampant in relationships. If you have been cheated on, its usually really doesn't have much to do with you. It's simply a choice made by the cheater.

Grounds for Love Rule #7: Stay Positive, This Too Shall Pass

When you are in the midst of the heartache and disappointment, it's hard to fathom, but this will indeed pass.

Having your heart broken can feel like the worst pain one can experience. You can literally feel broken, as though the end of the world is looming. Different people react differently, some people can recover with their self-esteem damaged, but intact. In some cases, however, the heart ache can push someone into an agonizing state of depression.

Numerous studies have shown that having your heart broken can in fact lead to depression. According to Psychology Today, a study involving 7000 people found that those who suffered "losses that involved lower self-esteem were twice as likely to trigger depression as ones that involved loss alone." Clearly there is no greater hit to one's self esteem than the person they love most in the world betraying their trust and choosing to be with someone else.

No one can deny your pain and you may need to take some time to feel that pain. Cry, get pissed off or however you need to emote, but you can't let it break you.

To still be carrying around the pain for a decade and a half, like my former client and leaving yourself unable to move forward with another relationship with a good guy, that's just self-imposed agony.

There has to be a statute of limitation on how long you let the actions of a selfish guy affect your life.

Reach out to a close friend or family. Don't isolate yourself, despite the fact that this will be your first inclination. Don't wallow and hide your head under a pillow or in a box of ice cream. Or, at least not too many boxes.

You are allowed to grieve the relationship, but don't be defeated by it. Seek solace in the company of people who truly love you.

This is not the time to be alone by yourself listening to nothing but the voice in your head and your heart pounding with ache. Get with people, talk it through. Vent if you must, but that too you have to let pass. The talk should be more positive—next steps—look on the bright side, kind of talk.

Try and stay away from friends with negative energy. You want to be with people who will have your back, but you don't want to surround yourself with people who will just feed your anger. That is not going to help you move forward if you just continually dwell on it. You will only become angrier.

Wipe him from your social media world. Sitting around looking at pictures or videos of the two of you from happier times is not the move right now. If eventually you manage to forgive and reconcile, that is a whole other book. For now delete him from your mind and that means wiping his impressions clean from your web life as well. Facebook, Instagram, Twitter, all of it. Don't even listen to songs that remind you of time together.

The less contact you have and the less you see of the cheating partner the easier the transition will be to getting past the hurt. Each day it will get easier and easier.

Steps to Take to Get Your Confidence Back:

1) Go back to the lab. Pull out your 'I Am Great' list. Remind yourself how awesome you are. The guy didn't make you awesome. You were awesome before you met him. You are awesome still. The list should include all the things that you

are proud of, it could be having gotten a good mark in a tough class or making the soccer team back in high school, anything that you had to achieve, regardless of how small you may think the achievement is. It could also include examples of good relationships that you have maintained over time. Perhaps a group of college friends that you are still close with, yes you can be proud of that too. Anything that takes effort that you have accomplished is something to be proud of. Recognizing and acknowledging what you are good at and even reflecting on small accomplishments you have made is a proven way to help rebuild confidence and having that list handy certainly helps.

2) Positive Affirmations. Only use positive affirmations, like; "I'll get through this!", "I can do this!" "I don't need him!", "I feel great!". Studies have shown that fully 95% of the way we feel about ourselves is determined by how we speak to ourselves throughout the day. Studies also show that if you do not speak in a positive way to yourself, people in general, are more inclined to *think* negatively to themselves and those negative thoughts end up shaping how we feel. You have to continue to feed your mind positive thoughts right now. Talk to yourself. Be your own 'hype man' and let those thoughts

grow and take over your mind and subsequently your emotions.

3) Positive Visualization. Create a clear picture in your mind of what you want in your ideal life. Make it detailed and replay that picture over and over in your mind. To get better emotionally, you have to get better in your head first. Positive affirmations and positive visualizations will get your mind in the right space and your emotions will undoubtedly follow. Feed your mind continually with positive content by listening to podcasts or other audio while you drive, workout or prior to going to bed. Absorb positive digital content online. All of these things will help to put your mind in a better place, as will hanging out with just positive people. This is no time to join an online group of women who got cheated on, certainly not if its just a bunch of people venting and angry, hating men. Stay around positive people who have a positive outlook. Avoid negative people. They can't help you right now, they will just drag you down into a sea of anger and depression.

4) Inspire yourself. Feed your mind inspirational stories. There is a saying that I always draw on, when times get tough. 'People complain about having no shoes, until they see the

man that has no feet.' Its normal to get caught up in our own world and think that our own problems are the largest that exist. In reality, there are always people who are suffering more. Read stories, books, magazine articles that are inspirational, educational or up lifting. By feeding your mind these stories, you will feel better about your own situation and have a more positive outlook and feel more confident about your life.

5) Replace him with Healthy Habits: This is a great time to take stock of your health and wellness habits. Start focusing on eating healthy foods. Maybe tweak your diet a bit if necessary. It's a good time to make those types of changes. Many women use this type of event to propel themselves forward into a healthier lifestyle. Start with your diet, eat healthier and more natural foods. A nutritional and healthier diet will have immediate effects on how you feel and think. Tag team that with working out regularly. It doesn't have to be thirty minutes in the gym five or six days a week. It can be just ten minutes per day. Just get moving. In fact, commit to just working out ten minutes per day, five days a week and you will be amazed on how good that makes you feel. Exercising releases endorphins. Endorphins make you feel

good. If you just do ten minutes a day, it will make you feel good. If you feel good, you will soon be doing fifteen minutes, then twenty. Start with ten minutes. Feel good. It can be anything, lift some weights. Go for a quick walk. Just get moving. Poor health habits and a lack of exercise predispose us to having negative emotions. Stifle those emotions by eating healthier and get your body moving.

6) Focus on things that make you happy, things that you are good at. Nothing regains one's confidence like success. Work on things where you can quickly gets some wins to build that positive momentum. Set some attainable goals and get them accomplished. Further, it doesn't even have to be accomplishment oriented, simply think about what you like doing in your spare time. Is it going for walks? Is it reading fiction novels? Is it going bird watching? Whatever it is, now is the time to do those things. Clear your calendar and make time for things that please you, things that bring you joy and make you happy. Do those things right now.

7) Hold your head up. Confidence starts with a mindset but your body and behavior can seduce your mind into thinking you are confident. Its starts with posture. Don't hang your head. Walk with good posture, shoulders back, head up.

Researchers from Ohio State University found that hunching over at your desk or slouching when you walk around can make you feel less confident and more insecure. Pull your stomach in and pull your shoulders back. Walk like you are one of the Avengers. Not the Hulk though, he tends to slouch. Along with better posture, put a smile on your face. If someone says "How are you?" Don't answer, "I'm alright". Instead, say, "I'm great!!" "Excellent!" If it happens often enough, you will start to believe it. Try it. Just by adjusting your body language a little bit you will definitely feel more confident. If you catch yourself, hanging your head or with bad posture, fix it. Stand up straight, head up, open up to the world.

8) Make eye contact. Look at people, not everyone in the world knows you have been cheated on and even those who do, are not going to be judging you as a result of it. You want people to embrace you, not feel sorry for you. Look people in the eyes. This comes more naturally when you are feeling good about yourself, feeling confident and on top of your game, but its urgent to look people in the eyes especially when you are feeling down about yourself. It projects self-confidence.

9) Look the part. Get out of the old sweatpants. Dress up. Go out. Go party. The distraction and good energy around you will help to heal you and jump start your self-esteem. Get some friends who like to party and spend some time with them. Laugh. To quote Proposition Joe from the tv show, The Wire, "Look the part, be the part." As one purveyor of sartorial splendor once said, "a man tells the world how he feels about himself by the way he dresses." I assume there has to be a similar quote regarding women. Get dressed up and get out so people can see you.

10) Wear confidence, like an armour. Confidence can be something you put on. Even if you are not yet confident, you can certainly act as though you are. You can fool yourself into feeling better, it's been scientifically proven. It then becomes a part of you, in the way you move, talk, feel, the energy you give off. Armour up.

11) Reclaim your life by staying positive. It has been well documented that whatever you expect to happen, really expect to happen with confidence, quite often does happen in your life. Expect the best for yourself. Don't sell yourself short. Always expect the best for yourself. Expect to be

successful in life and it usually materializes that way. Expect to meet great people who will add to your life and you will.

12) Laugh. Watch some funny movies, like Barbershop 1, or Rush Hour 2. But definitely don't watch Barbershop 2 or Rush Hour 3. You need humour right now and you'd be hard pressed to find any in those last two films. Laughing is probably what you need most of all. Laughing instantly shifts your mood and lets you, at least temporarily, forget what ails you. Laughter can cure stress, pain and heartache. Above and beyond everything else mentioned above in this section, nothing makes you feel better, quicker, than laughing. Laughter distracts you, allows you to release anger and heals your heart. Laughing promotes both physical and emotional health. It's been proven that laughing: Relaxes the body; Boosts the immune system; Releases endorphins; Increases blood flow; and even helps to lose weight. It's been suggested that if you laugh ten to fifteen minutes a day you would lose 40 calories a day, which over the course of a year would result in losing three to four pounds. Laugh.

What you shouldn't do however is over eat or drink too much. That will only lead to you becoming sadder.

It's still going to be hard to get past the betrayal and move on either with or without the person. Being cheated on can be an overwhelming thing to experience, but it really can be a good thing in the long run. It may have saved you from investing more years and then being betrayed later in the relationship after you had devoted more emotionally or financially.

As I stated, this can also be the launching pad to propel you to rediscover your own self, devoid of a running mate. Channel the opportunity in a positive way and you may be surprised how you can thrive. People are flawed. It's part of the human condition. The guy cheated. You have to accept it and move on.

If you do the things I've advised, you will begin to feel better in time. Look on the bright side, sometimes a betrayal ends up being the catalyst to end a relationship that really wasn't going anywhere.

Sometimes people stay in relationships just because its familiar. They know they are not inspired by the relationship. They know that it's not really their dream scenario, but they are comfortable. It's what they know. It's what they have.

When they have been cheated on, it often gives them the impetus to end the relationship. Quite often people move on and end up finding someone else who is actually better for them. Use the betrayal as a springboard, rise like a phoenix from the ashes of that bad relationship and propel yourself forward.

Think about all the things you may have wanted to do, but were not able to do because the relationship didn't allow for it. Now is your chance to go for it. Introduce yourself to some new experiences in your life. Things that you were being held back from doing, now is the time to do them.

It's still not going to be easy, but it will get better as every day passes.

Chapter Three

Moving On

Choosing Better

You don't want to rush into the next relationship. Give yourself enough time, but once you feel you are ready then you will want to make better choices in men going forward.

I have a friend who is always romantically frustrated. After she had gotten her divorce, the next three guys she got involved with, each time she felt they "were the one." Three times she either moved in with them or moved them in. Not once did she get a prenuptial or co-habitation agreement. Three times it ended up in disaster, costing her money and heartache.

She is a great girl who had married young and had never been alone by herself very much. After the divorce, she struggled with being by herself, so she welcomed new guys and quickly partnered with them, even though to her friends it was clear they were not a good fit for her. She never took anyone's advice and each time, she ended up losing more and more.

To her friends it became apparent she had been choosing the same guy every time. He may have come in a different shape, with hair a little less or more, but in terms of personality and characteristics it's as though she picked them all from the same conveyor belt.

The first thing I told her was she needed to find herself a Relationship Coach and she needed to ask herself a series of questions and they are as follows:

1) Do I really know what I want in a man?

You would be surprised how many women have never given this simple question any thought. But if you don't know what you want in a man, how will you know where to find him and how will you even know how to identify him. Write it down or at least discuss with a relationship coach or close friend what you want in a man. What type of characteristics are most important. Is it humour, stability, physical attraction? If you know exactly what you want, you are more inclined to find it and most importantly you will recognize it when it appears.

2) What will I absolutely not accept in a man?

Just as crucial to knowing what you want in a man, is knowing what you will not accept. Make a list of things that are absolute non-starters with you; Drug user, married guy, etc. Whatever those characteristics are, stick with them. Don't allow someone to charm you into making exceptions, you will only regret it later. Stick to your boundaries.

3) Who am I and what do I bring to the table?

Women tend to be more nurturing and accommodating than men. As a result, they will be more likely to settle and accepting of things that don't really fit within the parameters they set. That's not the way to go about choosing a guy. You have to know your worth and the value you bring to a relationship. By knowing that, you are less likely to settle with just anyone. You will be more inclined to wait for someone who truly fits you. Reflect on your 'I am Great List" and don't settle.

4) Am I looking for love in all the wrong places?

As the saying goes, "If you always do what you've always done. You'll always get what you've always got." To avoid meeting the same type of guys, change where you are looking for them. Go to different places. Change the dating sites too. Change your online profile. Change is good.

5) Am I giving off the right vibe to attract the right guys?

While we are talking about change. Maybe you need to change up your game too.

How is your look or style helping or hurting your appeal? Is it conducive to attracting the kind of men you are hoping to meet?

6) Do I seem desperate?

Good guys aren't generally going to be attracted to desperate women. Are you just running to the next man to replace the last man or because you can't stand being single? That's not a good look and almost certainly will end up in failed relationships. The more time you spend with guys who aren't right for you just means less time you are available for potentially meeting the right type of men.

7) Do I like renovation projects?

Some women know that certain guys are bad for them, but are convinced that they can change them, it's a full-scale renovation project. This never works. People are who they are. You can't change them. No one can change anyone. Further, trying to change a grown man is foolish and futile. Deal with men who are already what you want. Otherwise, like most reno projects, it will be too much work, too costly and it won't end well.

Grounds for Love Rule #8: Build it up slowly.

Solid Relationships that endure are usually the ones that are built slowly and grow over time. If it starts like an inferno fuelled solely by passion and sex, eventually that foundation will burn out. There has to be more to it if you are looking for something to survive the stresses of everyday life and temptations from other people.

Use your head, don't just follow your heart. The heart might want what the heart wants, but the heart has never been the savviest evaluator of men.

Ease up a little, take your time going into new relationships. Make sure the guy is worth the emotional investment before you push all your chips to the centre of the table.

Moving On

There has to be a balance of head and heart when it comes to assessing new men in your life. One without the other leaves a flawed evaluating system. Don't be overwhelmed with the attraction that is present at the beginning of most relationships. You also need logical assessment, to see if things can really work with the guy.

Are you compatible? Do you have shared goals and beliefs? Does this guy really fit me? These key questions have to be answered in the early stages and you won't even get to those questions if you are caught up in the sex and passion at the beginning. Sex and passion are great, just keep your head involved as well.

One former divorce client of mine married a much younger woman. He already had kids and told her that he didn't want any more children. This was all discussed before they got married. She said she was fine with that and just wanted him. Years later into the marriage she changed her mind. They divorced.

They should never had gotten that far. They knew they were not compatible, but got caught up in the heat and passion and chose to ignore what their head was shouting to them both. A costly divorce was the result.

Things to Look for In a Man:

There are certain consistent qualities that every woman should look for in a guy they want to be with long term.

- He understands that you are not perfect. He has to love you not just for your good qualities but he has to understand that you will have flaws and he has to accept those too.
- He makes you feel safe. He can be counted on. He has your back and is there when you need him most. Anyone can hang with you when things are all good, but life throws curve balls at times, you need to be investing in someone who will be there when times get rough. Will he make sacrifices for you?
- He always treats you with respect. Not just when times are good. Anyone can do that. But when his work takes a downturn or if his favorite team blows a 3-1 lead in the playoffs, the respect still has to be there. Certain lines cannot be crossed and that respect line is such a line. Respect is a must.
- He has similar beliefs and values that you do. Doesn't mean you have to agree on everything, but the key things are a must or there will be problems later.

- He should be selfless. It can't be all about his happiness. He has to care about making you happy as well. When a man truly cares about you, he makes your happiness a priority in the relationship and does whatever he can to please you, sometimes at the expense of his own wants and desire.
- He communicates. As we have discussed earlier, men are notoriously poor communicators in relationships. Your man has to be able to talk to you when things are rough or if he is going through a tough time, or if there is an issue. Often men talk to everyone but their woman about how they feel about the relationship. They talk to their friends, the bartender or even the Uber driver about things instead of coming home and talking to you. Every relationship will have issues and obstacles, the communication has to be there for it to survive. If one partner just holds in their discontent and let it fester, the relationship is doomed to fail. The only way to get through tough times are to talk the issues out with each other.
- He has to be honest about the commitment to you. Lots of guys can recognize when they meet someone they know is special and they want to be with. Some

of those same guys will still be reluctant to commit to an exclusive relationship. They may want you, but still want to be free to see other people. You need a man who is honest about his desire. Does he just want to be with you? Does he want to be truly committed? This has to be discussed and you have to be explicit in your language in terms of what commitment means to you. He has to be able to be honest about what his true desires are as well.

- He is willing to put in effort. Even if two people meet and are ideal for each other and they have the same values and desires, there will still be some effort needed at times. I don't believe that a relationship needs to be capital W work. I believe that if you actually meet the right person for you then things can run pretty smoothly, but even then, some effort will still be necessary. There will still be sacrifices, but you won't mind the sacrifice. He won't mind either and things will flow. But even in the best relationship, the waters can get bumpy at times. You need to make sure the guy is willing to make the effort to make this thing work, if necessary.

Red Flags

Women tend to be more intuitive than men. Numerous studies have confirmed that women are better able to read other people's emotions than men are. Quite often in a relationship those same intuition will be going off like an alarm, like a Spidey sense and women just choose to ignore it. If we are talking about a normal guy, the red flags are usually there. When I say 'normal' I am excluding world class con artists who can fool anybody. Under normal circumstances the red flags are there but the forgiving nature of women often compel them to ignore it. Instead they focus on the things they like about the guy, even while alarm bells are sounding off.

Grounds for Love Rule #9: Trust Your Instincts.

There are key red flags that should never be ignored.
- **Lack of Trust**. You feel as though this is not someone you can trust. This is a non-starter. There is nothing more important than trust in a relationship.

Trust entails you feeling safe and secure with him. When he tells you something you believe him. You are not worrying about where he is and who he is with. You can't be with someone that you are constantly worry about what's "really going on". That's no way to live. Lots of women drive themselves crazy obsessing over their partner because of a lack of trust. If alarm bells are going off early in the relationship, it's probably for a good reason. Obviously, there are exceptions. Sometimes women who get cheated on by one man, have problems trusting *any* man. But for the most part, trust your intuition, especially early on in the relationship before you are too emotionally invested.

- **Good Sex and Nothing Else**. Good sex can sustain a relationship for a good while, but only for so long. Eventually you are gonna have to talk to each other. Sex is a key part of a good relationship, but there has to be more involved if this is a long-term project that you hope will grow. Lots of women get caught up in the initial stages with a new guy because the sex is great and maybe that's what they need at the time.

Moving On

But, generally speaking, eventually you are going to need something more. For a relationship to last, it has to go deeper than just great sex. Unless that's the relationship you want. But just having great sex with somebody eventually does get old too. So many people have relationships and never truly know each other. They only ever get to a surface level. The sex is good and they never get past that. Then when something happens and they say to themselves, "I never really knew you." No, you didn't, because you never made it a priority to get to know the person. For a relationship to have stamina you will need more. You should know your man better than you know anyone else. If you just know him on a surface level then what is special about that? Most people in your life you will only know on a shallow level. The person you are most intimate with should know you deeper, beyond just sex. Open up with him. Entice him to open up to you. If he is reluctant to do so, even after you have made a real attempt then clearly, he doesn't want to get any closer with you. If that's the case, then that's a sign that you can't ignore. Don't settle, if sex is all he wants, while you want much more then that's a conflict that has to be dealt with.

- **Lack of Respect**. Like lack of trust, a lack of respect is a major red flag. If he exhibits a lack of respect early in the relationship, get rid of him. The early stages of the relationship are when most men are on their absolute best behaviour. If he is already showing you a lack of respect, then the relationship is doomed. He is showing you who he is and you should listen. Further, even if he shows a lack of respect to other people, don't wait for your turn. You need to be with a man who respects you. If the respect isn't there early, it's not going to be there late. Respect has to be all encompassing and consistent. He can't show it from time to time. Respect is a constant and he should be generous with it. It should extend to not just you, but respecting what you do for a living, respect what your interests are, your friends, your family and your beliefs. This is also a non-starter. You cannot spend your time trying to build a life with a guy who shows you a lack of respect. That's beyond foolish.

- **He Doesn't Inspire You.** If you are going to spend so much of your time with someone, it should be someone who inspires you to be your best. So many women stay with a guy they don't look up to, guys who don't inspire them to be the best they can be. Quite often its the opposite. They stay with men who bring out the worst in them. Your man should be championing you, building your confidence and encouraging you to ascend. Instead, in many relationships women allow their man to bring them down. Some women become someone they don't even recognize as they become consumed with a lack of trust, jealousy and insecurity as a result of being in a toxic relationship. I've seen it many times. It's like they lose their own identity and become less themselves and more of an extension of the guy and whatever frailties and faults he may have. You have got to hold on to who you are and if the guy does not make you better then what is the point of being with him. Let's take sports for example. A good teammate is supposed to make you better. They are not supposed to tear you down or make you lose your confidence.

They should inspire you, make you *more* confident because you know they have your back. When you are in a relationship with a guy who brings out your worst, you have to recognize it and bail. There's no salvaging that. You need to get far away from it. Let somebody else sort him out. Being with a man who makes you insecure and uncertain, a man who makes you angry often is no way to spend your time living. It's unnecessary. At times women are so wrapped up in the relationship they feel as though they have to stay and work things through. Sometimes they may be addicted to part of the relationship. The sex may be good or the guy may have lots of money or you may have history with him. But what kind of future is it going to be. Not a good one. Get with a man who uplifts you and is devoted to making you better instead of sucking the life out of you and turning you into a person lesser than who you actually are.

- **He's a Blamer.** This guy doesn't take responsibilities for his actions or his lot in life. Instead he is quick to blame everyone else, his family, his ex-wife, you, anyone but himself. Pay attention early, if you hear him blaming everyone for everything, that is a sure red flag that this guy shirks responsibility and will likely blame you for anything that goes wrong with the relationship as well. He will do anything but admit that he is wrong or that anything was his fault. People are who they are. If you see him putting blame on other people, you better believe that the blame will make its way around to you eventually. Better to be with someone who fully understands that a relationship involves two people, therefore two people are responsible to support and maintain the partnership. It can't be just left on one person to shoulder the blame. A guy who doesn't take responsibility, that's just a weak characteristic and not conducive to being a good partner. That's not someone you can rely on and you can be certain that he will turn on you to point fingers at you and tell you what you are lacking in. If things go wrong for him at any point down the road, he will find a way to place the blame on you.

- **Temper**. Probably doesn't need to be said, but I'll say it anyway. Violence in any relationship can't be tolerated. There has to be an absolute zero tolerance on any man being physically abusive with any woman. Domestic violence permeates the social fabric of our society. Its been well documented that in the North America alone, more than three women are killed every single day by a partner or former partner. Countless women suffer physical, verbal and/or emotional abuse at the hands of men. You cannot expose yourself to abuse. Any man who is an abuser is beyond your scope of ability to 'fix'. Let the cops sort them out. Any man who even gets in your face in an intimidating way should be avoided as that is often a precursor to an escalation of violence. Don't allow yourself to be a victim. Don't spend time with men who are abusive in anyway. You deserve better than that. I know the issues surrounding domestic violence is often complex in terms of why many women stay in the situation, but at least early in the relationship, before you are sucked into his vortex of violence, if you notice the guy has a temper or gets angry quickly then that is a guy who should be avoided at all cost. You cant give men like that a second chance, abuse is unforgivable and its pretty much guaranteed that if someone hits you once they will do it again. If they lose their temper and get in your face in an intimidating manner once, then it will likely happen again. They are just exhibiting their natural instinct and behaviour. Stay clear of men who explode easily. Avoid men who are violent towards women or have a history of violence towards women. Don't fall into the trap of thinking "he won't be like that with me". You are wrong, people are just who they are. If someone is violent with one woman. It's highly likely that he will be violent with other women as well. Violence against women is a disease, once a man has it, he always has it. It may lay dormant for a while, but it will resurface in time. Any guy who exhibits a short fuse or who has anger management problems is not someone to be around.

A lot of times women will know that a guy is just not the right guy for them to be with. Yet they would rather be with someone than be single and having to search again, so they settle. In their head and sometimes their heart they know that the relationship is going nowhere but they stay in it and work with it and invariably are miserable in it.

Life is short, don't give years of your life to someone who doesn't treat you right or doesn't show you love and respect. You have to believe that you deserve better than that. When you meet a guy who makes you feel secure and safe, someone you can trust and there is mutual respect, those are foundational pillars on which to build a long term relationship. Anything less and you are just setting yourself up for failure down the road.

Grounds for Love Rule #10: Don't Settle.

One of the very first clients who came to me regarding a divorce, was a woman who had been with this actor for years. It's the typical story, the relationship started out very good, he was excited to be with her, treated her well initially and was exciting to be around. She moved in with him very early into the relationship. From the beginning, it wasn't really a balanced partnership and she didn't feel empowered in it. He made all the money and though he was generous to her, he always made a point of reminding her that he was the actor, he was making the money and she was merely the waitress who dreamt of opening a bed and breakfast in Niagara-on-the-Lake.

He was disrespectful and diminished her dreams. He made her feel foolish for even thinking it possible. He determined that her role was to play supporting actress in his life and nothing more.

Then he got into drugs and turned further into an egomaniacal control freak and even escalated to being physically abusive to her. Essentially, he grew to treat her like owned property. This went on for a couple of years before she finally decided she wanted to leave the situation. But despite the abuse, she felt her sole identity in life now, was being with him. All their friends that they hung out with, were actually friends of his that she had come to know through him. All her original friends, no longer came around as they hated to see how she allowed herself to be treated by him. Still, all that being said, it took another three years for her to finally come and see a lawyer. Five years it took her before she finally took action.

By then she had been with him for ten years and built her whole life around him. She had thought this was the guy she was going to have kids with and thought, nearing forty, it was just too late for her to get out and meet someone else in time to have children and a family life.

She eventually did get out of the relationship. Shortly thereafter she moved to Mexico to work at a resort and to forget about the guy. A few years later she ended up meeting a great man. He is a builder who works in South America. They ended up getting married and they have been together for over a decade now. Together they own a small resort down south. It's a thriving business and they have a great love affair and she has never been happier. In fact, I have not met a better couple more suited for each other. I still see them every couple of years and have gone south to visit them on occasion. She never did get the kids, but she does have some beautiful horses, a couple of dogs and even a goat. Why the goat? I'm not certain. But she is literally always happy and I am so happy for her.

Had she not had the courage, she would never have left the abusive relationship to find true love. Her husband treats her like a treasure. He truly does. He shows her the utmost respect. When you see them out together, it's as though they are on their first date still. He values her contribution to their business. The idea was hers. He's a builder, so he built it and she runs the resort. Her dream has literally come true and its growing, as they are now looking to expand and own a second property soon. She also consults other people in starting up small resort businesses.

I think someone is out there for everyone. I think women often don't have the patience or courage to make themselves available to the right people. Sometimes you are in a bad relationship and it's a grind and you feel stuck. So people stay and days turn into months, turn into a decade. When you look back at the relationship you would be hard pressed to find a couple of consistently happy days that you can even string together. If you are not happy, you should leave the relationship and find someone better for you. They're out there.

The client I just mentioned, it took her a couple of years to rebuild her confidence after being with the actor. He had broken her self-confidence and eroded her self-esteem over time until she had none. She felt as though this was her lot in life, to follow along playing a bit-part in his dream at the expense of her own wants and desires. She endured the abuse. She endured the disrespect and was never happy for very long.

Once she met her current husband she realized what a true partnership can be and she hasn't looked back, except to say, "I should have gotten out of there earlier." Which is the familiar lament for most divorced women.

I'd be remiss however were I not to mention that the actor, shortly after she left him, misfortune rained down on him like flames from Drogon. He spiralled into serious drug abuse. As a result, he ended up being unemployable for years. He lost all his money and most of his friends. He ended up having a kid with a woman he barely knew. She has him seemingly, in a never-ending parade to court seeking more and more child support.

Karma.

Found the Guy. How to Keep Him.

Don't bait and switch. Be who you are when he met you. Don't turn into someone else. Be confident and be open. That being said, being open doesn't mean you necessarily have to tell the guy absolutely everything about your past. If you had a couple wild years in University or if you dated a rock band, not every guy can really digest that. That kind of stuff is on "a need to know basis only" and most men don't really need to know. Best to keep that on the down low. As the saying goes, "What happens backstage at a rock concert, stays in Vegas." Let's stay focused on the new relationship and the future ahead.

Here are some key strategies to keep a man.

- Keep your friends. A lot of times when women get involved with a new guy, they dump their friends and replace them with the new man and his friends. That's not necessarily attractive to a man. A good man, wants a woman who has her own life going on, with her own friends as well. You don't want to come off as being too needy and dropping all your friends. That is a sure sign to a guy that you could become too needy. That's too much pressure for him to handle, especially early in the relationship.
- Let it breath. At the beginning don't spend every single day with him. Allow the relationship to breath. It also shows the guy that you have a life beyond him and that makes you more powerful in the relationship and lends itself to a more balanced relationship.
- Be complimentary to other women. This shows your man that you are confident in your own skin. It is unattractive to hear a woman dissing every other woman. Its a clear sign of a lack of confidence. Do the opposite, let him see that you are not threatened by other attractive women. That's powerful to a man.

- Don't call or text him incessantly. Remember guys like to pursue. I am not saying you should play games, but let him be the one who reaches out most often. Guys like that better.

Grounds for Love Rule #11: No Innuendo.

You've gotta set the parameters and standards in the relationship. You have to let guys know from the start what you like and what you don't. You have to let us know how you expect to be treated. It's at the start of the relationship that these things should be tabled. If you don't set guidelines guys will just think they have the run of the place and can do anything.

I have a Great Dane named Barkley. When I saw Barkley climbing up on my leather couch for the first time, right away I reprimanded him. I didn't let him get away with it once and get comfortable. I know the dog doesn't like water in his face, so I kept a spray water bottle nearby and I'd spray him. Very quickly Barkley learned to stay off the couch.

Moving On

With guys, I'm not suggesting you use the spray bottle necessarily, but you have to set the tone of the relationship right from the beginning. Guys will push the envelope as far as you let us, but if you establish the parameters right from the start, a guy will usually adhere to the expectations.

Letting the guy know the ground rules in plain language doesn't mean disrespecting him. It means letting him know unequivocally what you will or won't stand for.

Numerous men who have cheated told me that they didn't think their wives would leave them over it. They thought she would be "pissed off" or "mad, but wouldn't break up our family over some piece-of-ass on the side".

In most cases those guys were wrong and the women did leave. In the cases where the women did in fact stay after finding out about the infidelity, the relationship will never be the same, and though she may have physically stayed, emotionally she has checked out as the trust will no longer be there.

I am good friends with this terrific artist named Anne-Marie. We went to university together. We never dated. Anne-Marie has a rule with all of her friends. She won't stand for profanity in conversation. She doesn't like it and she's let it be known to every one of her friends not to curse around her. You know what? We don't. And if a swear word happens to slip out around her, I feel compelled to apologize. Why? Anne Marie set the parameters early and everyone respects it.

Treat your man like Barkley. You have to let men know explicitly what is not acceptable. You have to have that conversation. Don't assume guys fully understand. Be explicit and let them know what the rules are.

Grounds for Love Rule #12: Keep it hot.

There's a famous quote that guys kick around in male locker rooms in gyms everywhere. I'm not sure who to attribute it to, but it goes, "Every time you see a beautiful woman. There is some guy who is bored having sex with her."

Just due to the fact that your man sees you all the time, he will in all likelihood become complacent. It's just human nature. People in relationships, after a time, tend to take each other for granted.

In the early stages of a relationship, people are more inclined to be spontaneous about their actions and are less predictable.

Moving On

They are more playful, respectful and thoughtful. They are less inclined to be put off or bothered by trivial things.

One woman came to me and wanted to divorce her husband because he complained about her purchasing grated cheese. He wanted her to buy the cheese and then grate it. I guess that would be cheaper. Now clearly there had to be more for her wanting to leave the relationship than the cheese, but like grating cheese, little arguments over time add up. It starts out small at first, but eventually you are looking at a mountain of cheesy complaints. In the beginning of a relationship, the man would hardly complain about the cheese for a couple of reasons:

- He wouldn't feel as though he has the jurisdiction yet and he would hardly want to do anything to put her off.
- He probably wouldn't be focused on trivial things like grated cheese, while he is still swooning over her romantically.

But the moment a couple let their relationship transition into the 'comfort zone', that's when people start taking liberties. Now, normally one would associate comfort as a good thing. We like a comfortable bed. We want the car we drive to be comfortable. You may have a favorite chair at home that you comfortably recline in. But when it comes to your relationship, the comfort zone is not something you should embrace. I mean think about it. If someone says to you that there are two parties happening tonight and you are invited to both. One is filled with the most exciting people possible. The other are some people who will make you feel comfortable. Most of you will undoubtedly pick the exciting party.

Well in fact, your relationship most likely started out in the exciting party and one or both of you have allowed it to drift out to the dreaded comfort zone. In that zone is where complacency and boredom set in.

Let me be clear, becoming comfortable with your partner is a good thing. But having the whole relationship just rest in that zone with no balance of excitement or spontaneity just sucks the life out of a once exciting romance.

Once people have gotten past the newness of the relationship and have decided that this is someone they want to be with long term, they quite often erroneously shift their mindset from excitement and lust to one of comfort and predictability.

For men, they may physically reside in the comfort zone with you, in fact they are often the one to get their first. But once

Moving On

there and comfortable, most men still have the desire for excitement and newness.

Most couples after a time, perform sex the same day, same time, same position. As one client told me, "My husband has sex with me once every quarter. I can set my watch on it."

In the comfort zone, there is no longer any effort to come up with new ways, positions, ideas, nothing. As a result, the relationship has no air being provided to it and needs to be resuscitated. But by then someone, has started looking somewhere else for excitement.

You have to fight the predictability of the comfort zone. Don't let your relationship dry up from lack of air.

If the guy is cheating then the woman on the side has all the advantages. Every time your man is going to see her, she is dressed for the occasion. He never sees her hanging around the house in old sweats or worn out underwear. She is always ready and waiting and excited to hook up. He never sees her when she has a cold with a runny nose or is a mess sick with the flu. Every time he gets with her, she is on point, geared up, scented and giving him her full attention. That is a huge advantage.

The landscape is clearly skewed in her favour and guys are a sucker for that. They don't take into the consideration the fact that anyone can pull that off for 2 hours a week. They suspend the reality that you may have gotten the flu by nurturing the two flu ridden toddlers that you have with them. Guys often just see what's in front of them and they feed on it.

There are ways that you can regain the home field advantage and it really doesn't take that much work. People always lament about how a relationship is a lot of work, but from the man's perspective, we really don't need much. Guys are easy, just throw us a bone every now and then:

- Be spontaneous from time to time. Change things up.
- Once in a while meet him at the door geared up in something sexy.
- Don't just save the perfume for when you are going to work or out with girlfriends. Sometimes just put scent on for no other reason than to terrorize him.
- Anything out of the ordinary or different, a guy will eat it up.
- Get the TV out of the bedroom. If it's there then you may both end up watching Game of Thrones reruns instead of handling your business.

Moving On

Remember how the relationship was when it started? Bring back some of that excitement, tease him a little, just be different. Shock your man out of the comfort zone.

Grounds for Love Rule #13: Be Your Man's Kate and Edith too.

Men want the classy girl in public, but they may want something else altogether when it comes to sex. Communicate with your man. Let him know what you like sexually that he does. Let him know what you'd like to try.

Ask him what he wants. Some couples stay together for years and never really please each other sexually. Sometimes the guy thinks he is hitting a home run in bed, while his wife may be thinking 'that's more like a pop fly'. Yet they will go on like this forever without either person willing to discuss how to make it better or hotter.

When a guy strays, most of the time it's not that he even finds the other woman more attractive. He just finds her different and because the lover on the side relationship is based around sex, the man tends to communicate more clearly about what he wants sexually and the lover on the side tends to do so as well. They talk about sex more. They let each other know what they like more.

Before each rendezvous the foreplay starts with explicit communication, via phone, texts or even FaceTime calls about what each of them are looking forward to on the upcoming tryst.

Divorce lawyers make a ton of extra money these days as their clients often send them pages and pages of illicit communication they have discovered.

Almost always the woman is shocked that her 'strong silent type' is articulating like a dub poet to his 'side piece' in ways he has never done with her.

You have to open up the lines of communication. Don't leave it to the man. Ask him questions while you are in bed, ask him what he likes. Tell him what you like. Guys will be more open to communicate then, while you have their undivided attention. As opposed to you saying to him "Hey, we have to talk" in the middle of the NBA Finals.

Some men are more insightful and gather that women are complex creatures with the capacity to be layered. But that often takes communicating and men are notoriously bad communicators, especially with their wives.

Moving On

Ironically, a man will tell an anonymous table dancer his life story over six Heinekens and a cascade of slow jams, but often the same guy will go months before telling his own wife that he lost his job.

Be the one to throw on the white business shirt and red pumps tonight.

- Rent a stripper pole, (Yeah you can rent them) put on your best song and do a dance for your man
- Alternatively, sit him in a chair and do a lap dance for him

Remind him of how electric you made him feel at the beginning of the relationship. The feelings are most likely still there. They are just lying dormant. Many couples rediscover themselves years into a relationship. Bring out the stripper in you. Men like strippers because they act confident. Turn the lights down low. Pick a nice song, be confident and tantalize him.

- Costume Change; Dress up for him occasionally, something scandalous. Men are more visually inspired than women. Throw on something sexy once in a while. Inject some excitement into the relationship.

- Make Up; Throw a little make up on. Once a couple enters the comfort zone, one of the first things that women eschew is make up. They will get made up for work or for girl's night out but neglect to do it just simply for their man.
- Talk the Talk; Talk in bed. If you normally don't say much, say something dirty to him. Guys eat that up, especially if it's not a normal part of your routine. Let him know how he feels. Call him Big Poppa. Call him Medium Size Poppa. Just say something.
- Mirror, Mirror on The Wall; Make love in front of a mirror. Just seeing even parts of each other in a mirror moving together will be erotic, especially if this is new to you both.
- Old School: Get back to something you may have stopped doing. Many couples start off with a no-holds barred attitude sexually, but as they get into the comfort zone they stop doing the things that drove each other crazy. Pull out your old school moves.
- Scene Change: Break up the same room, same routine monotony. Do it in the kitchen, the garage, or do it on

the balcony with a slight risk of being seen. Just don't get arrested.

- Bring out the props: Visit a sex shop, pick up a couple of toys that you may like to try out. If you are too shy to go to a sex shop, then go to the supermarket and pick up some honey, chocolate syrup or some whip cream.

You have to keep it hot, don't just sit in the comfort zone and let the relationship wither away. Give your man his Kate and Edith too.

Confidence Empowers Success

More than anything else, what I'd like you to take from this book is the importance of being confident. I like to say 'Confidence Empowers Success, in business, relationships and life.'

If you are confident in your relationship, you know your worth. You know you are a person of value and you have high self-esteem. That empowers you. If you are empowered that means you are more likely to be in a balanced relationship and a balanced relationship is more likely to be successful. Confidence empowers success.

Grounds for Love

There is nothing more attractive than a person who exudes confidence. If you are confident, people want to be with you and they want to be around you. The way we view ourselves is the most determining factor as to how others view us.

The more self-confident we are, the more likely we are to succeed not just in business, but in our personal relationships as well. Be confident in who you are. Make an 'I am Great List' for moments when your confidence is down. Everyone experiences a lack of confidence at times.

In 2016, I took my son to a series of NBA playoff games to watch our hometown team the Toronto Raptors go farther than they ever had in the playoffs at that time. They made it all the way to the Eastern Conference Finals that year only to lose to LeBron James while he played for Cleveland.

For much of the playoffs, the Raptor's best player, NBA All Star, Kyle Lowry struggled. I mean, he was missing layups and wide-open shots. This went on for several games during their run.

When finally asked about it, Lowry was candid. "Right now, I'm struggling with my confidence." He said.

Here was one of the top twenty basketball players in the world where close to a billion people actively play the sport in

Moving On

some capacity, yet he too was experiencing struggles with confidence and was candid enough to admit as much.

His teammates had his back in the media, openly giving him support at a time he really needed it. No one piled on him and said, 'Lowry needs to do a better job right now".

As I said earlier, being in a good relationship is like being part of a team, a two-person team. If one partner is struggling with their confidence, the other person is supposed to pick them up and uplift them to make them better.

At no time is your teammate or partner supposed to assail your confidence. Don't stay with a man who attacks your confidence and tries to bring you down.

Pick men who are worthy of you. Don't sell yourself short. You are worthy of being treated right and being happy. Set a standard on how you want men to treat you and they will. If they don't then keep it moving. They clearly don't deserve you.

Relationships can be tough at times, but it's during those tough times that people often exhibit who they really are. Even when things get stressful, there has to be a level of love and respect.

Grounds for Love

Too often people attack those they love, spewing venom that they wouldn't consider directing at strangers. That's not right. That's not healthy and it shouldn't be accepted.

If you find the right person, they will treat you the right way. Even when they are upset or angry, certain lines of decorum should never be crossed. That's just respect and love. Don't settle for anything less.

Manufactured by Amazon.ca
Acheson, AB